Saffron Splash
By Ann Huang

UnCollected Press

Cover Art: Ali Irons & Nigel Kuzimski; Cover Photo: Eric Stoner

Book Design by: Rebekah Ferrell

UnCollected Press
8320 Main Street, 2nd Floor
Ellicott City, MD 21043

For more books by UnCollected Press:
www.therawartreview.com

First Edition 2025
ISBN: 979-8-9905585-7-1

Dearest~

That *exit* moment

at the gate. You exclaimed

about our dreams being stopped

at the _ grown-up rate: the shadow

up-close

and

realities sway.

Imagine the sunrise *saffron*.

Wind gusts the same way

about the same one as last summer,

swifter – I see everything before me

a line made of our touch

a stanza built by our stories

a poem breathes our love

as the night shortens

we hold onto what we belong.

Contents

IV Cali-Choir

V The Natural

I.   Ancestral Stories

A Fable was Born

Before the storm had eastward blown,
The goddess pressed on and
The dirt lied down.

Age is the goddess who drifts alone.
The goddess forgets,
Age remembers.
The hearts of the poem excite.

The poet lives and dies,
The goddess leaves the space behind,
The hearts of the poem are in the space.
I tune my mind into them.

Light in the Snow

You left behind a green dress
in your youth. It insulated
your happiness.

Your beliefs blended in with your time,
hairy, colorful, patient
from
the sympathy of hard-won truths &
mauve pink flowers.

Light drawing you near—

men longing
beyond
their jungles
& lost trajectories—

the marked cross
appeared as a vogue woman
rising to your psyche.

After the Kale 蓝

With gray flip flops, you sunk
under the bottom of your mom's
tote at forty years old.

After the wedding.
After the old house.
After the kale 蓝 .

After the chopsticks in the kitchen.
After the cat's litter.
After the monkey fish.

After the sky
around you, there was the sky
above you.

Through the
lean years that prompted you to give up,
your willowy figure--
you often saw success
was unlike this.

Morning Rose

Up the warm, autumn morning
A fat, red sun consumed the skin.
The leaves were dreamlike red

And the ubiquitous sun swam in dawn.
Red leaves, knocking at the latch,
And she sat in a white lace dress,
Her soft skinny body, alluring...

Surrounded by the bright windows to the streets,
Eventually she startled,
The fireflies in her mind.

Remembering, "The joy has wound up with allure."
You followed her waist;
The pear fruits nudged at the gate;

When is too much not enough, for pleasure?
When is enough too much?
To despair...

For the Steam

For the steam you fancy in distressed light, and listen as if outside
a box.
How the moon like the rain-brushed moans and the trance of red-
laced nymphs
And the wind through keyholes
                                        Inter-lacing and
connecting as it disrupts,
Like a hostess of tender nights with gold chains on her heart.

And you mean the steam: a real part of the human soul would
come,
    you search for a life that would connect so
                                                    and all
frailty it knows,
And a mind that would flow with myopic shadows and wandering
truths.

Poetry Lessons for the Living
after BIRDMAN

Father's flannel chocolate briefcase
Empty without cards.

A tall tin cup of tea.

The brim opening
on one-man show.

Sad quintessence,
clay and clouds.

The bitter poem
of wealth

Rising alongside you
unlike
the nostalgia
from an earthy life.

II. The Daily

The Dreamer

Your old Mexican blanket
has a saddle print in serape stripes.
There is no open thread or lint
on its vintage weave and style.
All afternoon it sits alone
on the couch's buttoned cushion.
You rub your body against it
and sob in the evening.
Then you find it
ascending around your hair,
lilting about the windows
and near the bed,
dancing passionately
with knots of brighter stripes!
You listen to it
in your dreamy state,
out of flamboyant joy.

Obsession

Open the door by closing it.
It's for the best—

[and love
trapped]

Let nobody see
where you are.

While I stay with you,
you will be a legend.

An old argument—
dancing alone.

The tide will show us
for as long as we live

I'm thinking
There is nothing dangerous

Quintessential

The woman before me

was unaware of your

most delightful jokes.

You inclined through dreams

not knowingly—

filling in yourself...

You, my guardian angel,

looking over me

with your tenderness!

You love me

quintessentially.

Bright Waters

Bright morning waters in the East,
When sunrise warmed like a body
Of saffron splash painted for everyone.
New peace warriors in heaven, close to
Some casual designers on earth,
Which freshened the shadows of the moon,
You illuminated—as if all afternoon
Was illuminating, and all things, reborn.

Somewhere Along the Way

You've always contemplated afterwards
    somewhere along the way was blissful.
The fast pinch of a lifetime happiness
    that you do not treasure anymore.

It should be easy to know better;
    That-deemed happy soul truly knows
Wishes and reliance on mistrusts and bravery,
    not to mention heartaches and damages.

The morning is somewhat bright,
    and the evening somewhat dim,
and all this new love that has given you—
    a wishful well-being.

You have seen afterwards
    somewhere along the way was blissful,
then overcome yourself in forgiveness—
    you will learn from it some more.

Melt

Sometime today it stopped, and sometime after noon
    you could not eat; the uneasy heat
Against the dwindled possibility of an unexpected poem,
    Against the cards on the table in a room with a view.
And in the sky the bright sun loved you,
    Like a familiar body in firm nakedness
Hugged you tenderly, warmly, holy-grail style,
    And rested sweetly upon your blissful nape.
And hey, there was magic at dusk!
    The moving mist swirled at length,
The cloud, with a veil of silver overpowering the sky,
    The poetesses scribbled in the lonely heights.
And many people changed in many ways,
    You whom wondrous charm could only affect;
To me, the radiant were close by
    And you were soaked in the thirst for my fleet.

Life Remains

Life remains, by simplified nails
on which places had themselves hanging.
Life cracks in the full start of the morning
when nothing of its own weight is daydreaming.
Life has gathered some moments near seniority.
Before that, life was young, feathery and fast.

Could make it up to someone some more,
Could it be exposed in the crowd, could walk, could watch.
Could it lean in to whom to love
when it left no time to remember.

Destiny Embraces Many:

The people that harm
you the most
aren't those you alienate.
Many nodded.
"Destiny is not empathetic."

Going from one extreme to another:

lurking after a horn
learning flamenco
teaching the dog to fetch
enjoying a fleeting speck of time
imagining a future this beautiful

To undress the dress, unbutton a blouse--
customarily for the beloved.

The body insidiously accompanies
the rhythms of page-turning.

III.   The Artist

Diurnal Descent

After you demanded everything
From luxury, the morning
Arrived to readjust

an endurance from non-season, you were
Flowing to the moon, and

You forgot that the cornfields
Would spoil you, animals
Carved on the stones, your guidance

Would take away the contemporary myths
And the windows from the future
randomly to the river. You barely

knew
Words, you were not
removed from the earlier years

Of produce. You did
Pronounce yourself

As a hook
would look after the prey. And you never
Made your projections

Beyond your caresses. On the lawn
By the time you stayed
And beyond

Rising
after Richard Robbin's GIRL RISING

She fell asleep in Midsummer to touch morning,
                          from black and dreaming
        of the night:
The sun, expanded and thickened to the curve of a woman's thighs
exposed to
        the mirror,
And the pairing of a parody life, loving in vain and enormous.

A Wasp often grabbed her, a fortune lured & dampened her,
                quiet and   dormant.

That was not the prize, the favorable life, sought after, presented
simply,
United us
By words, the world and rising.

All afternoon you are wondering

This is what you tell yourself: you bundle all the feelings together, like in a melting pot.

You swear by the questions you have refused to ask. Their thrashing turns light as air.

You have brief inklings of a scam. There are people you had to drop, and they do seek answers. An inkling does no good to one, if one loves—

A mind is more than an ocean. A mindset is an inkling. A stubborn one is a scam. All afternoon you are wondering.

That Such and So

Whether or not your lover is an algae
      Sinking in the bottom of the sea,

You would open the car windows
      To assure her air.

Whether or not you cared for her rebirth at the
      Tip of the trees,

You remember to paint her there
      When you'd fly high!

Habit(at)

You follow the summer heat.
All evergreens are taking the toll.
You lack good

Karma in life. The steady inclines,
The well-planned years from a gazer's
Path find you at the cliff's edge
When you can't leave without your back

Turning. Lovers, with clean
Sheets and pillows/of inward peace.

IV. Cali-Choir

The Choir

You repudiate industrial machines but your thoughts are often
over-stressed,
amplified, and overpowered. Vera Wang
Velvet, Valentino, all contemporary West Coast dolls
with their sweetheart breasts and poker smiles.

Their gold nymph mothers, lusted from the massage tables,
glossy, their husbands busied with colorful Hanky Panky

and who does you good in front of churches
and philanthropy and fundraising. When

will you think like the literary luminaire
many years earlier? Whoever

involved you in a relationship that is deeper
than a lover's grasp, you hardly notice your patience, your bonding

heart. Your mind is beautiful, with no reservations.

My Eternally Beloved
after Beethoven's Love Letter

moonstruck daffodils
that mirrored her soul, your heart
blessed, broad with breathlessness &
blissful melancholy of a given life. Unsterblichen,
Geliebten, your sisters shouted out
to tell you that your chest was a wall,
which was to new found romances. They turned
door knob fully to the brightest colors
to the wayward, what they thought
you needed. That was only one part of your life.

Sarah

Those are the moments that keep you alive.
You whisper to the candle light.
You eat cake
Beyond a close proximity—
The reservoir bank
In the way that age moves on.
You are young except for those who are younger
Over and over.

And to be glued on to each other
Both of us like shards awaiting to be glued on,

That was not what age enlisted.
The planters you refused to receive
Had tea tree oil and berry currants, and
The crescent springs you created upon yourself.

Without Words

Will you dry off from an illuminated tomorrow,
  you wholehearted know when the giraffe will bellow
    By brown facades and orchid-shaped lights?
    Under the windmill, next to a cat, you run
accompanied by dusk winds; strongly close by,
  Gone loosely your train of thoughts to be a golden viola,
    Without unanswered chords of a fairy tale,
  When dusk winds arrive, you are forced to go.
My indigo trade is hard with blending.
    I fancy you, the words jump and drop
Like big, enveloping hugs of the sky;
    Our bodies are silent, sea-crafted to the fissures—
A silver goblet, a yellow rose, a tangerine, what will that be?
    Words resurface—while you rekindle the idea of them.

You are in more than every presence

The colors of winter pond
make your look early-spring.
A chisel of magic ice
on your hair, you warm
the whole room with a smile.
The moon singles you out till morning's rise
and you brink
at someone's purpose of life.
The clouds top out and
every other one is present.
You take in all the loving,
The unspoiled roads being your palm.

Somewhere

Somewhere you read a good poem
—only it is not surreal,
It was not meant for us,
And you left the words in its baggage;
Devils! Some endured.
You laughed, "Go away, sweet feelings!"
And they cried.
They stayed on
Till they became air
Breathable in between you and me.

Opening Ceremony

What brightens your face, what makes you smile?
What do you know about my incline through life and dreams?
What is my light?

How bright it was, what was it?

Who wears the magic shorts, they are not here, and an open space
is a bright spot. Gray and pink are not green, orange and blue are
not yellow, red is rouge, an arrow is of
one color. A dot melts it. A dot simply melts it.

The Dot of Light

On your face
your shadows
feel your eyes close
to adventure
sacred in the late afternoon
and lost in light
what were you doing?
Where will it take us
the dot of light
My deep ocean
Our synchronization
ending in
demarcation

....

Entangled

There are new people:
Alchemical angels,
Bright angles,
And there are specks of old stuff,
Paper and dust,
An unexpected person,
Membrane on a keypad,
Memories through an oeuvre;
Words, let them flow
Patience: when I can't cry.
I will never be over you
Saint and lenient one!
There are secrets,
Filled nuclei,
Soaked fringes,
Strengthening feeling,
And weakening lineage.

Sunset

The west is red as a rose.
Twelve steps—twin elusive porcelain limbs—are trusted
To the house. The smooth tulip trees soak
Up the short venue by a grain of salt—

Distant from the town and all the groaning trains—
Become gray and gray always, with smiles bitter
And slow. Start with the morning the moon blinks.

Down under the water is tumbling, a panel
Of shades. The west faces to pink awash,
And remains: now, eternally it seems,

Stalky streets, tulip bulbs, and twelve steps;
To the dryness of the trails up to the valleys,
The reluctant boxes, like home, stop apace.

Forever

The fish were quieter this evening,
tender, cheerful, anchoring their bright tails to coral.
It soothes you, now you knew it's Fall.
How do they know when to be a fool? /Primitive/
Mad fish, will you like to go where it runs deep?

Love Learned by Loving

"Dear love!" you mumble, "dear love!"
And the descendants of the men
Sigh through your singing, and the dolphins and whales
Serendipitously love what you make peace
With, earth's [one's] trivial identity. Cloudy strokes
Shake up the wetland; forest-trees
Unilaterally steep; birds follow, born; and amiss
Wild flowers, reborn daily to the desert bushes.
To tell the well-spent moon, which look
Forward to their renewing meaning. God of newness!
Give you a big cadence— and so much love,
As a slice of ocean that never diminishes to discontent
Through the age and sage.

Spent

We expand our lungs at sunrise,
strolling alongside the water
making ourselves connect to its aliveness:

about earthy things like flowers that
shall see their blossoms before wilting?
We hasten to climb onto the rocks

and find out how brightened at the seashore's
abruptness, the small proximity of
morning sun & its dwellers onto its length.

Venus.2

                                        Dragonfly in a gift
package
                                        a surreal one
                                        a poem
                                        a damsel
                                        two
                                        for joy
                                        filled and
                                        in no way to
think

                        you were happy when your
miserable _____ finished directing
        film   series
                        she showed you the innocence
                        and the sandstorm in the beach
                        about love and extension
                        for unconventional zest

In Praise of Love

You dig into the country dirt
when the garnets flow &

and the lovers attract
the wandering pigeons and dogs.

You lounge by the shrines of masons
and their spoons hallowed by insomnia

from the ocean of white sails
to the worn-out sky and tongues of cats.

She follows you to a meeting room,
luring the sunset
which pulses with love and laughter,

the strong shadow of dusk,
the sea dwellers.

Porch in the Rain

In the rain that blushes shady light
Fresh tuberoses miraculously melt,
And peonies bloom way too bright.
There is a feeling of calm night,
A sense of home,
An elevating whir of fruits and dandelions
That you never left unattended,
Centers of fine brittle beings,
And straight sails you often ran into only in dreams—

Your porch reckons,
Behind the coils of rain—
And reappears!

Sky Laurels

Garnet musk
melted with silver,
malt in the ocean
stamped with an enriched gain,

splashed afar to the poppy-seeds
from the tycoons' beaches:

my talks have been ignored by
surrounding dry weeds
and fought-for sky
and pleaded clouds
and unifying horizons.

Charming, narrow-pouted,
water upon shells,
when the plateau shields
so magnificently a spell
for a brighter tale!

Everything

A book of pleasure. A person of wine. The calling from nature.
Someone in that entangled beehive noticed—

unlike playmates under the eclipsed sun—
an old chapbook of synthetic carbon-hydrates

foreshadowed what future had shown—
at the end of the disconnected alchemy

a paranormal knowledge leaps and effects natural scenes.

When you have thought of "everything," a string of murmuring
contacts
will discharge the fitting to space.

Floating above the White Nube

You took in nothing that would bring you shadows

and hang only gray on the wall.

Blues and soft watermarks and whites.

The insatiable scribbles during the nights

embraced your cerebral stimulation and wit—

Elation, aren't you here?

Know until I am here and there isn't all I want.

Who did what tomorrow —felt short behind the light.

Traction

Listen to me carefully
go back to that moment
I was in the salon
everything was very confused
the car stopped

It was a sea lion
I was in the water
I saw a maze
we were kissing
we were in love
I saw the sea lion's head

My life started when I saw you there
Nothing before that mattered

Lasting Menace

The unscrupulously shaped tree stands tall,
Bewitched houses bloom in the fields,
And cast a shadow of the gray shabby throne—
Close to the banks where the monkeys run—
Thrilling goldfish who gleam sharply,
The near-sighted stars in the milky way of life.
So lasting in my blood are all beliefs,
Ethereal beauty, Age's mesmerizing,
All loves the eternal love inspires.
Immersed into the word's surreality,
We live beyond the concrete jungle, don't we?

Flagship

A bright sail
Like the reflection of a window
When the morning sun rose.
The sun then would golden its admiral thread
Beyond the morning sheers
And the nearby banks
For those mortal mariners.
The never-discoloring clouds.

Finale

The moon is emotional
But with a polished mind ...
Ordinary boys wrestling
Surrounded by the galaxies.
It is not the sky's show ...
The sky has risen beyond the air ...
These incessant act out publicly,
Welcoming the shout of the dream.

From Distant Cities,

I tune my mind into them.
The heart of the poem in the space.
The goddess leaves the space behind,
The poet lives and dies,

The hearts of the poem excite.
Age remembers.
The goddess forgets,
Age is the goddess who drifts alone.

The dirt lay down.
The goddess pressed on and
Before the storm had eastward blown,
A fable was born.

Acknowledgements

A whole-heart appreciation to the editors of the following presses and publications for placing my poems with their candor/homes:

"After the Kale蓝" Featured on the World Poetry Day (March 13, 2023) in Moonstone Arts Center;

"Light in the Snow," "Morning Rose," "Destiny Embraces Many," and "Lasting Menace" Published in East Lit (June 2016);

"For the Steam" Featured in CSU Poetry Center's Open Book Poetry Competition;

"Entangled" Published in Alexandria Quarterly (October 2018);

"Sarah," and "From Distant Cities" Published on VerseWrights.com (June 2016);

"Finale" from the manuscript ***Saffron Splash*** Published in Straight Forward Poetry, Issue Ten (Available on Etsy);

Saffron Splash Named a Finalist for the 2018 Vella Chapbook Contest (October 2018);

Saffron Splash Selected as Semi-Finalist in Word Works' Washington Prize (June 2016);

Saffron Splash Selected as Finalist in the CSU Poetry Center's Open Book Poetry Competition, judged by Emily Kendal Frey, Siwar Masannat & Jon Woodward (June 2016).

Ann Huang is a multilingual Chinese American poet, filmmaker and visual artist based in Newport Beach, CA. Her award-winning poetry has been featured in *Denver Quarterly, Ruth Stone, Rue Scribe, Hunger Mountain, The Blue Mountain Review, The Elevation Review, Helen Lit Mag, The Florida Review, The Bare Life Review, The Bookends Review, Tiny Seed Journal, The Write Launch, Verse Wrights* and elsewhere. Huang is Ephemera's June Poet 2023. She is producing a limited art film series *Ann Huang Presents.* Find her work at AnnHuangPoetry.com and SaffronSplash.com. Twitter: @AnnYuHuang

Other works by Ann Huang
Love Rhythms (2012)
White Sails (2015)
Delicious and Alien (2017)
A Shaft of Light (2019)